David Del Tredici

Facts of Life

for Solo Guitar

Distributed By

www.boosey.com
www.halleonard.com

Published by Boosey & Hawkes, Inc.
229 West 28th Street, 11th Fl
New York, NY 10001

www.boosey.com

ISMN: 979-0-051-10761-2

Notesetting by David Nadal, Alessio Olivieri and Holly Druckman

Commissioned for David Leisner by John Jr. and James D'Addario,
Ralph Jackson, David Leisner and 13 friends.

First performed on April 29, 2010
at Symphony Space, New York, NY by David Leisner

FACTS OF LIFE

for solo guitar

I. First Things First 1
II. Fugue, My Fetish 9
III. Farewell, R.W. 17
IV. Flamenco Forever 21

Composed from November 1, 2009 to December 31, 2009

Revised: June 2012

COMPOSER'S NOTE

Though I have used the electric guitar in a recent song cycle (*A Field Manual*, 2008) and guitar–like instruments – the mandolin and banjo – in many of my *Alice* works, the thought of writing a solo guitar piece for such an accomplished artist as David Leisner filled me with trepidation. As it turned out, however, this was the happiest 'co-creative' experience of my composing career. David has a knack for turning my crude 'base' elements into pure guitar 'gold'.

Movement I, *First Things First*, is an adaptation of a piano piece for left hand alone. With little change, it fits quite naturally into the guitar range and technique. The movement has a discursive quality, ranges through many keys and includes an elaborate recapitulation not unlike the first movement of a Sonata–Allegro form. The principle material is an oscillating triplet figure which, in the middle section, takes on a Spanish flavor and at the end, a *cantabile* expressivity.

Following without pause is Movement II, *Fugue, My Fetish*. Another fact of my life is that I love to write fugues. This became an increased challenge with the guitar – an instrument not naturally given to counterpoint. On the other hand, there are the amazing Bach fugues for the lute and solo violin that inspired me.

After an introduction, a rising scale line, capped by a triplet figure, is the theme of a fast–moving, extensively developed fugue in three voices. It acts as a kind of scherzo movement.

Movement III, *Farewell, R.W.*, is the slow movement and 'soul' of the work. Tranquil, even ecstatic, it was inspired one afternoon by feelings surrounding my most recent relationship breakup – a sad fact of my life.

And, for the finale, there is *Fandango Forever* – the most elaborate and lengthy of the movements. It was conceived as an act of pure perversity. Early on, I was searching for musical ideas and asked David Leisner about what style guitar music he would *least* like me compose. Without hesitation he answered vehemently, "Spanish – it is so hackneyed!" I liked his intensity, took his words as a challenge and responded, laughing, "Then *that's* what the finale will be!" And so it was. My intention was to write completely idiomatic and highly virtuosic flamenco music – fast moving multi–string chords, seductive harmonies, triplet rhythms – even some indigenous percussive effects. I wanted this movement to seem inconceivable on any other instrument – except of course for the contrasting middle section, which is another of my knuckle–busting fugues. Irrepressible, the clangorous flamenco music returns and yields to an even more brilliantly virtuosic coda, capped finally by an outburst – from the guitarist himself!

The work is dedicated to David Leisner, my dear friend and peerless performer.

—David Del Tredici

EDITOR'S NOTE

Commissioning, editing, practicing and performing this work by David Del Tredici have accounted for some of the happiest, proudest moments of my performing career. I am deeply honored to have been involved in the creation of this masterpiece by my sometime composition and orchestration teacher, whom I regard as one of the great living composers. It was a collaboration of the deepest intensity. We got together at least once every week for three months to edit, re-arrange, revise and revise again. And after it was over, there were more revisions and then more. David Del Tredici's unerring ear and unstoppable quest for perfection led us through a labyrinthine journey that was, for me, an unforgettable, thrilling experience.

At its root, David Del Tredici's compositional instinct is contrapuntal. Writing counterpoint for the guitar, especially for a non–guitarist composer, is a difficult and impressive undertaking, well worth the effort, as it lends a rigorous integrity and depth to the work. There are many places in the piece where my fingering does not sustain every voice for its full value, but in all cases, I have retained in the score what the composer wrote. My goal was to strive for a balance between fidelity to the composer's intent and ease of playability. One of the reasons why the editing process took so much time was that this balance needed to be addressed over time, living with each movement and the entire piece as a whole, in order to arrive at the best possible solutions for endurance. With a composition this large and difficult, the spirit of compromise is paramount.

A word of caution to the player: be sure to note that accidentals (in the octave they occur) always carry throughout the measure. There are a number of places where, either because of the length of the measure or the complexity of the texture, a player may forget that a note has a sharp or flat earlier in the measure.

The composer understands that such a lengthy work may not always be played in its entirety. It is to be expected that guitarists might wish to excerpt the work in performance. Certainly, for example, the sublime third movement can and will stand on its own. Or singling out the fourth movement, which uses a common flamenco gesture as a springboard for a wildly imaginative ride that surprisingly veers into fugal territory, would be understandable. Or one might wish to isolate the clever, heartfelt and wondrous obsessions of the first two movements. However, for those intrepid enough to take on the entire piece, your considerable efforts will be endlessly rewarded, that is, if your experience is anything like mine.

—David Leisner

NOTATION GUIDE

Two types of harmonics are employed:

NATURAL HARMONICS – Sound at written pitch.
(diamond–shaped notehead): Fret and string are indicated.

ARTIFICIAL HARMONICS – Sound an octave higher than written,
(circle above the notehead): i.e. – the left hand fingers the written note.

⌒ all solid–line phrase markings are the composer's.

╭╌╮ indicates a left hand slur, suggested by the editor.

CIV_5 indicates a five string barre in the fourth position.

$_hCIV$ indicates a hinge barre in the fourth position.

`1 a dash prior to a left hand fingering indicates a guide finger.
(does not necessarily mean a glissando)

FACTS OF LIFE

I. First Things First

DAVID DEL TREDICI
(2009)
edited by David Leisner

979-0-051-10761-2

Allegro, con fuoco
ritard.
CV2
ff
l.v.
(ff)
f
Andante
p
p
f
p
CII2
CII2
f
f
f
p
CI3
f
f
f

With a Spanish flavor
CIII4
CII2
CX3
CX4
CVIII4
CVII4
CII4
CIII4
CIII4
CI4

accel. sempre
al.
Allegro (♩. = 116)
cresc.
Passionato

accel.

CIX5

80

CII3

f sempre

Cadenza

(CIX5)

83

(freely)

ff

(84)

ff

ff

(84)

CVI3

Allegro, con fuoco

CI3

(84)

(85)

fff

rit. **A tempo** **rit.**

88

p

f

Andante

93

pp

accel.
Allegro, con fuoco
CI5
CVI5
sub. riten.
accel.
cresc.

A tempo
113
f cantabile
117
CVI5
CVI2
(CVI2)
121
CVI
125
CIII4
CII5
(CII5)
129
CVII4
(CVII4)
133
CVI2
137
CVI2
hCIV
CX2
hCVIII
p subito
p sempre

dolce
dim. sempre
rit.
Andante
rit.
Andante
accel.
Allegro
ritard.
Andante
accel.
Allegro
dim.
ritard. al fine
attacca
April 14-21, 2009
New York City

II. FUGUE, MY FETISH

cresc. sempre
Allarg.
a tempo
accel. poco a poco
cresc.
poco
rit.
a tempo
a
poco

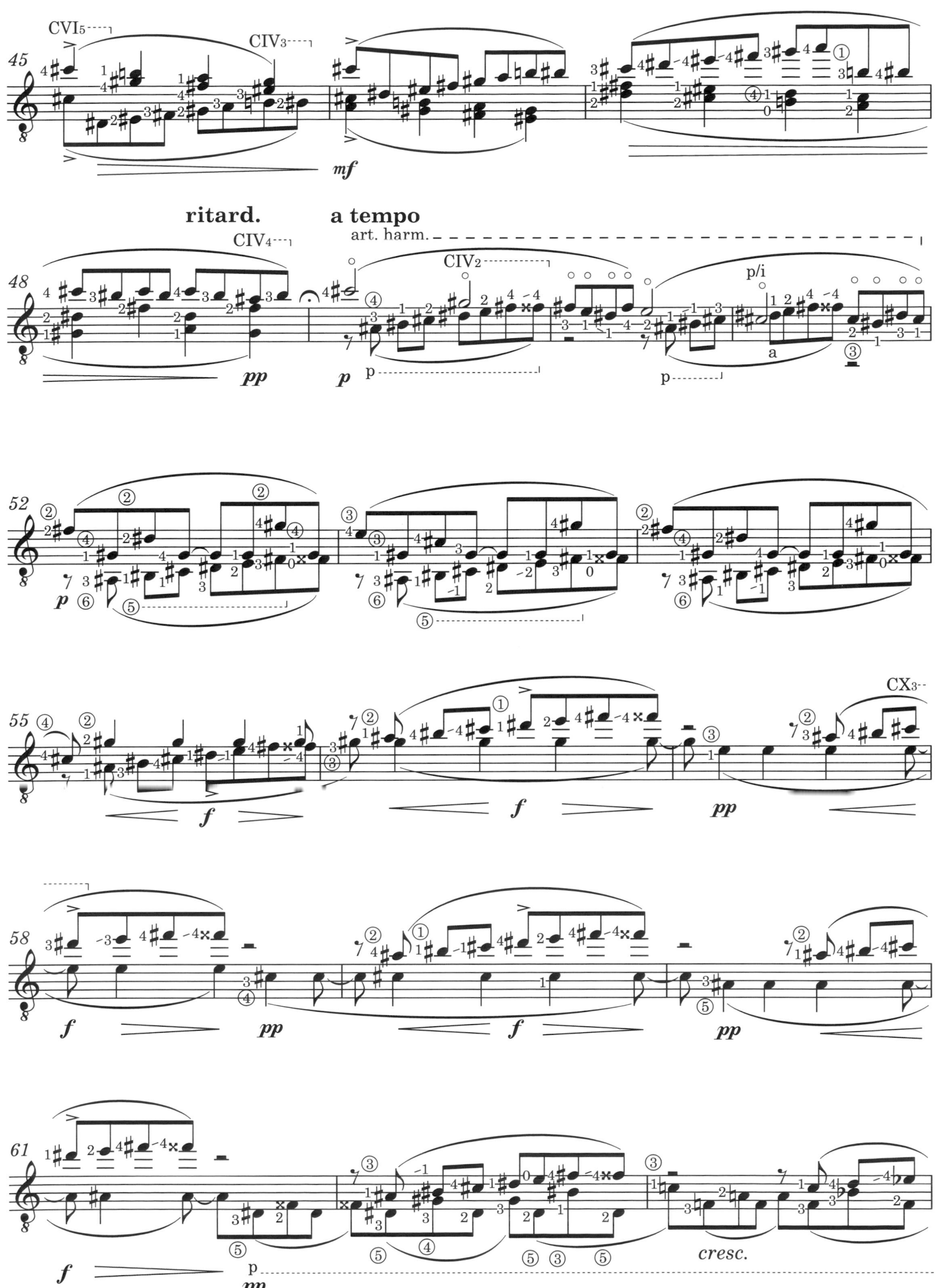
ritard.
a tempo
art. harm.
cresc.

rit.
a tempo
art. harm. 8va
64
(p)
f
p

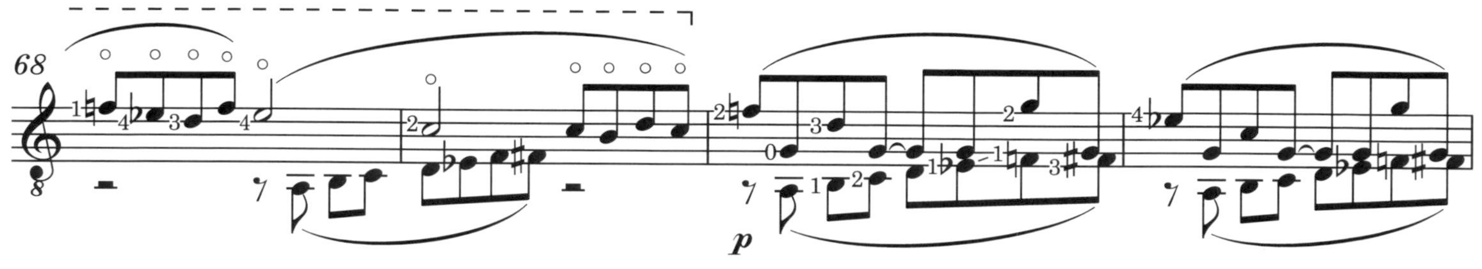
68
p

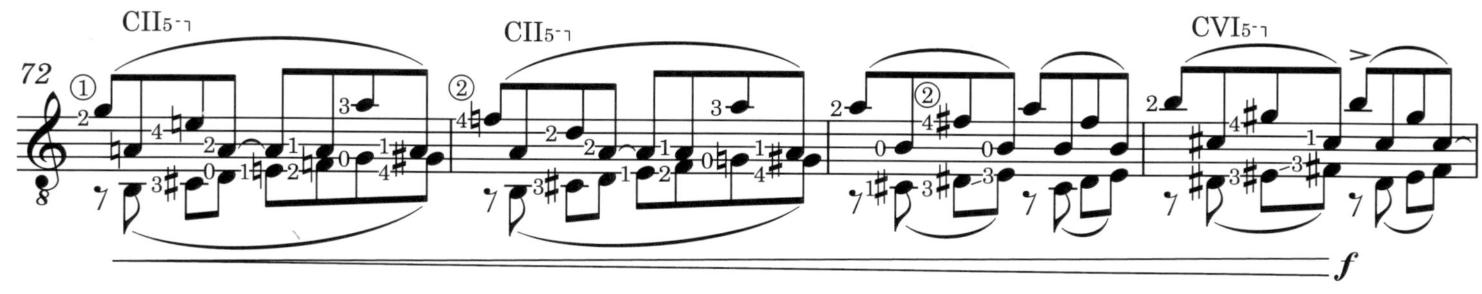
CII5
CII5
CVI5
72
f

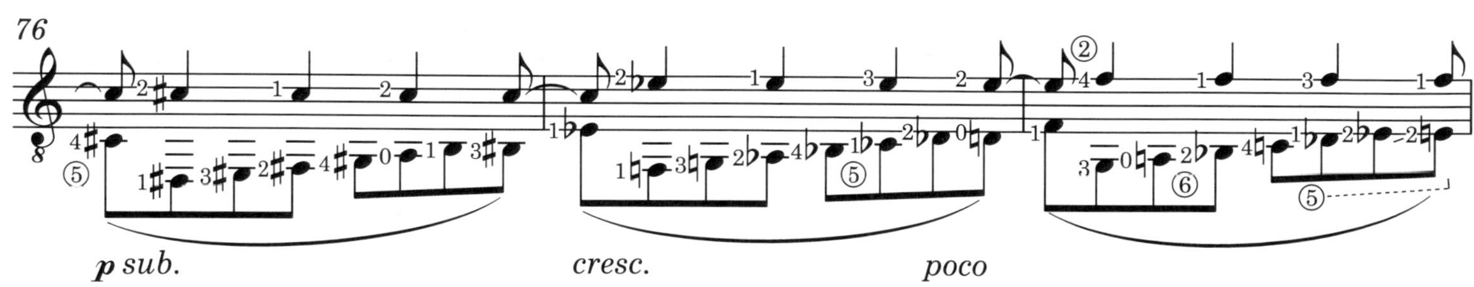
76
p sub.
cresc.
poco

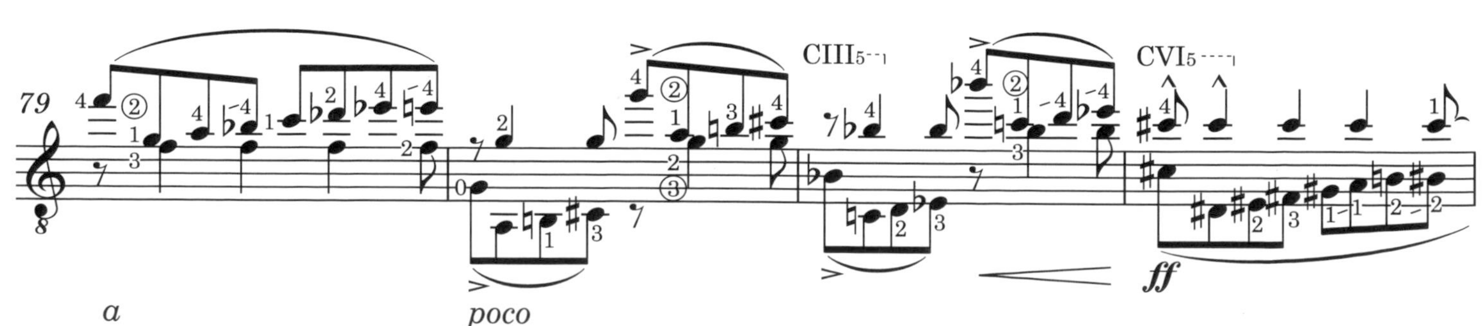
CIII5
CVI5
79
a
poco
ff

83
i m a
i a m
86
CIV2
p
p i p
89
CI2
cresc.
f
92
più f
CVIII4
ff
95
a i p p a i p p
m m
ff
CVI5
CVI4
CVIII5
CVIII4
p sub.
98
(CVIII4)
CVII3
f
p sub.

f sub.
p sub.
f sub.
p sub.
dim.
pp
cresc.
p sub.
p i m p p i m p
rit. accel. allarg.

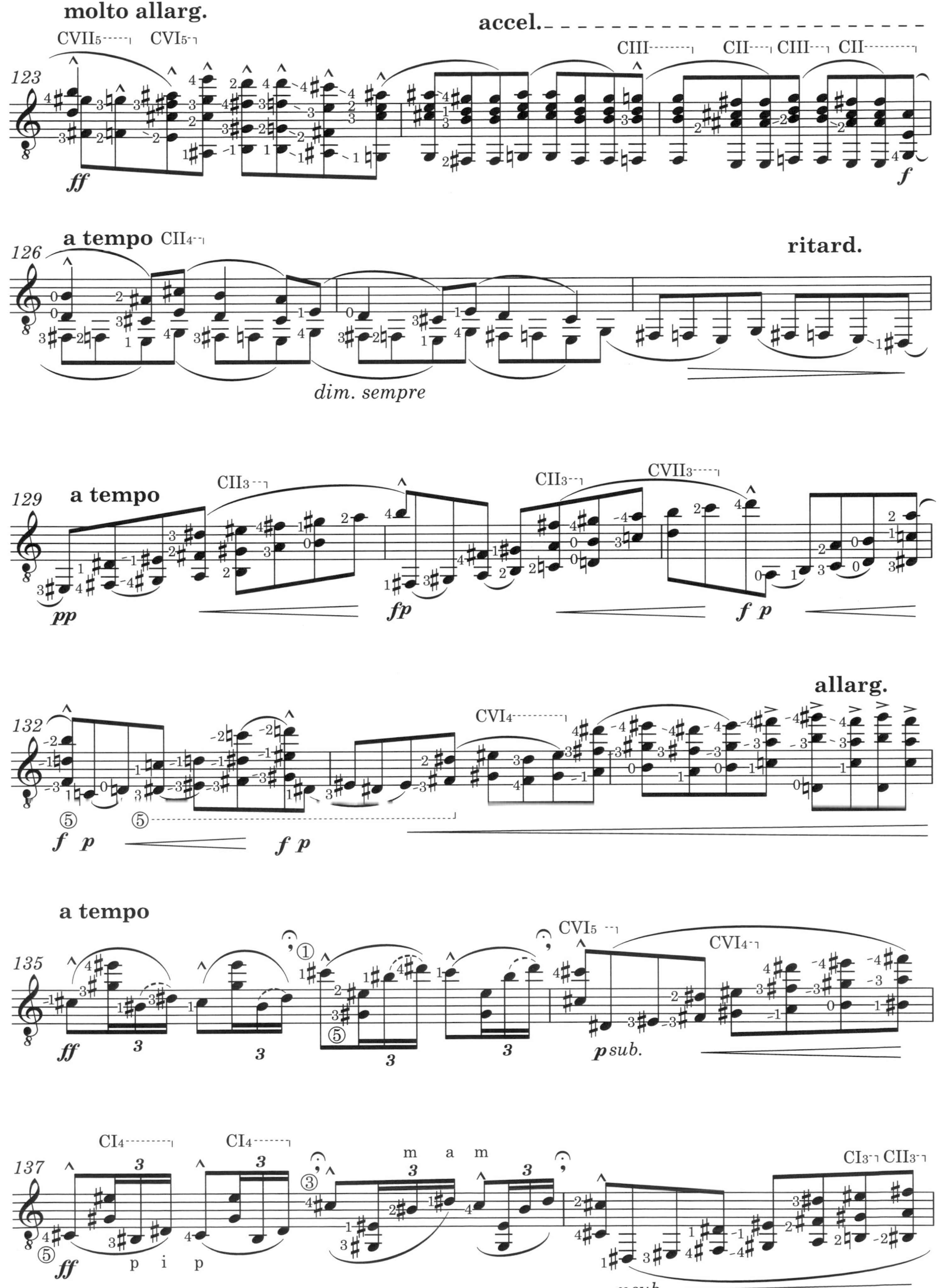
molto allarg.
accel.
a tempo
ritard.
dim. sempre
a tempo
allarg.
a tempo
p sub.
m a m
p i p
p sub.

October 20-24, 2009
New York City

III. FAREWELL, R.W.

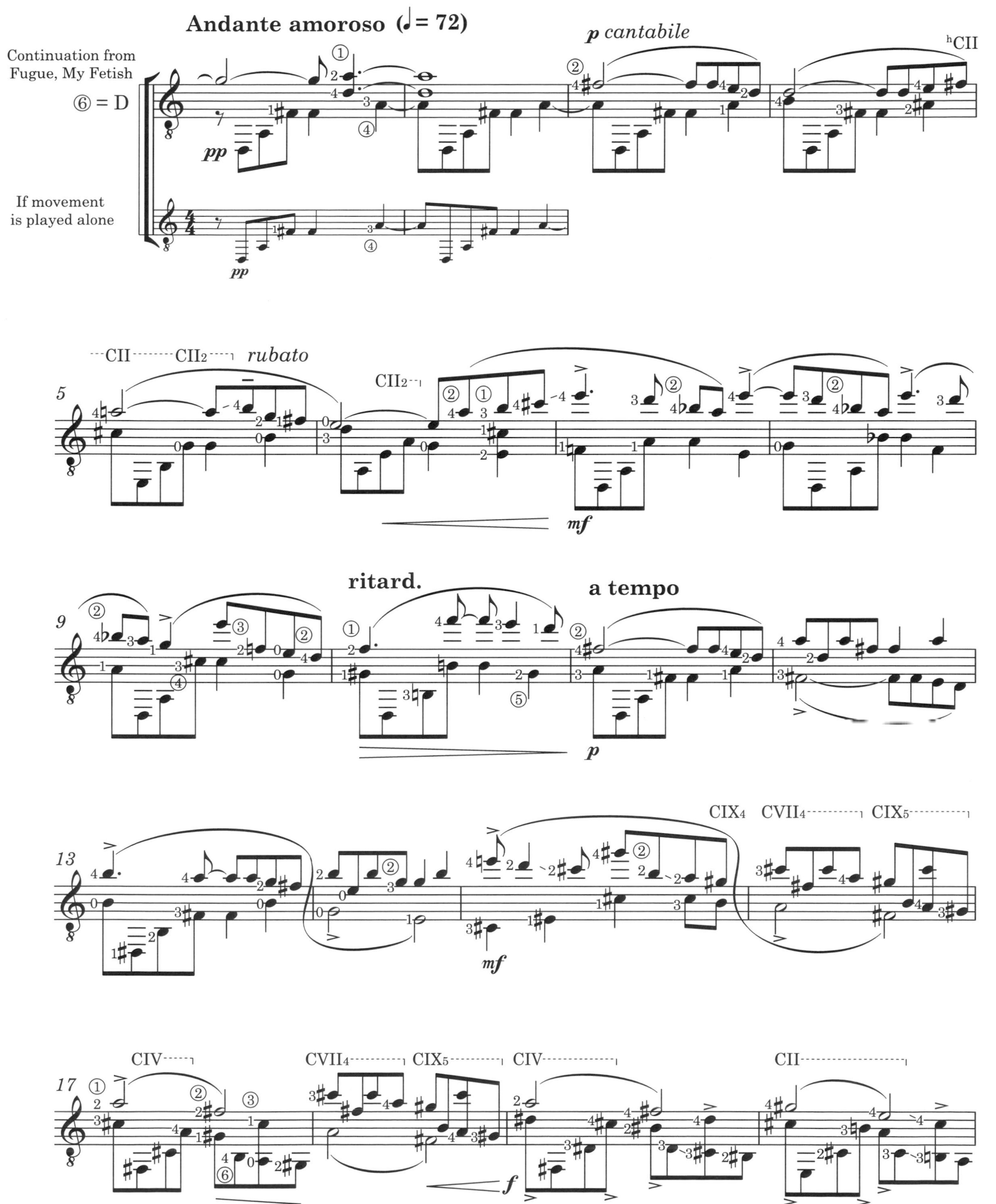

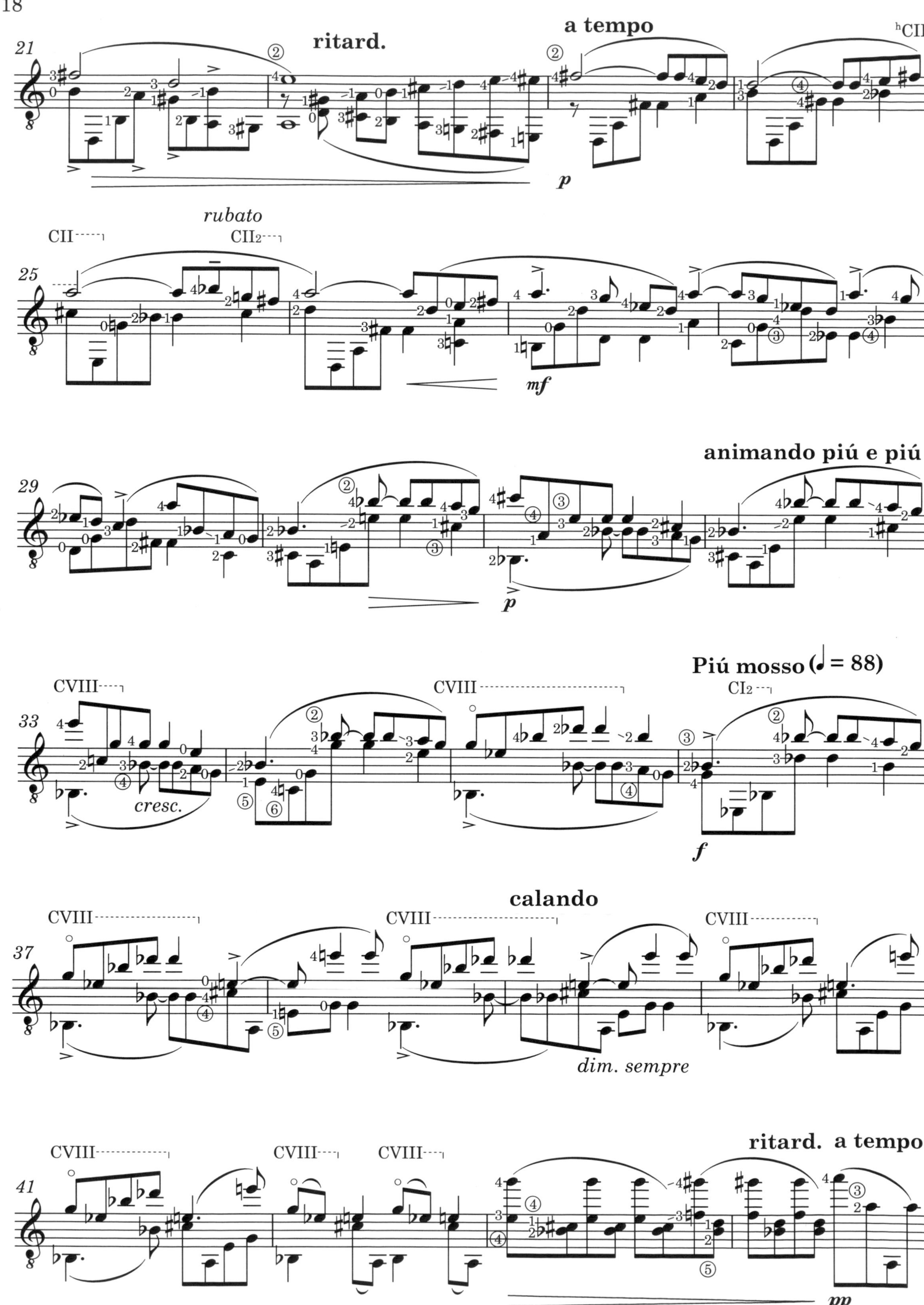
ritard.
a tempo
rubato
animando piú e piú
cresc.
Piú mosso (♩ = 88)
calando
dim. sempre
ritard. a tempo

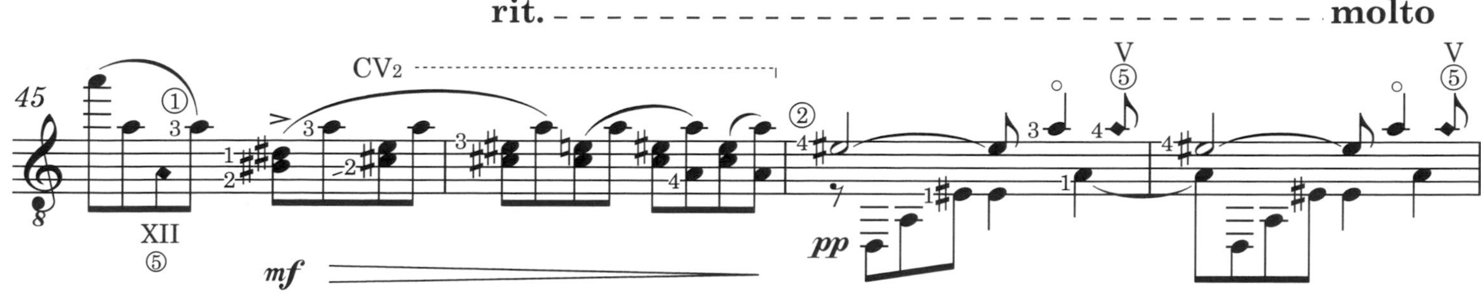
rit.
molto
45
CV2
XII
mf
pp

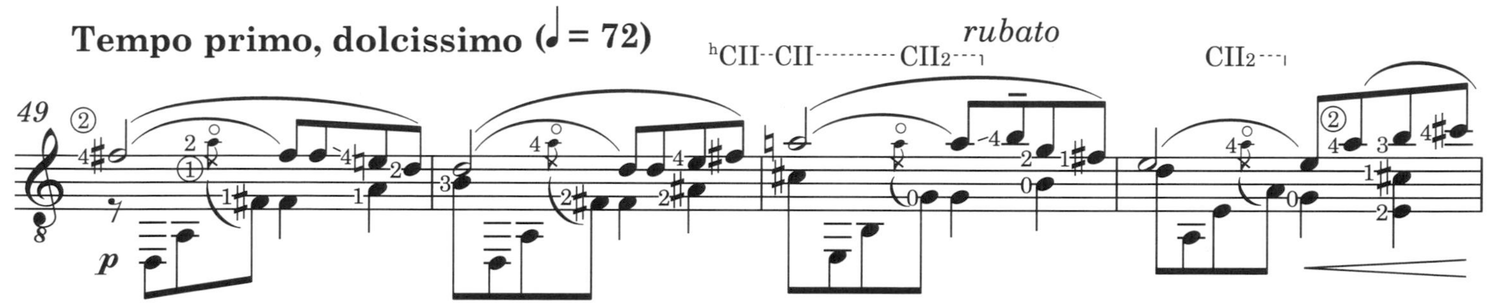
Tempo primo, dolcissimo (♩ = 72)
rubato
49
CII
CII2
p

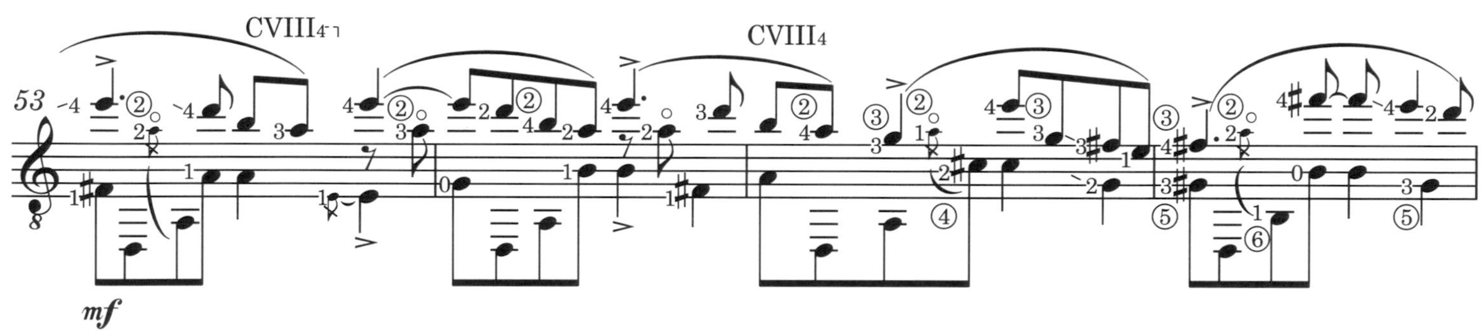
53
CVIII4
CVIII4
mf

ritard.
freely
57
p

a tempo
R.H.
XIX
61
f
mf

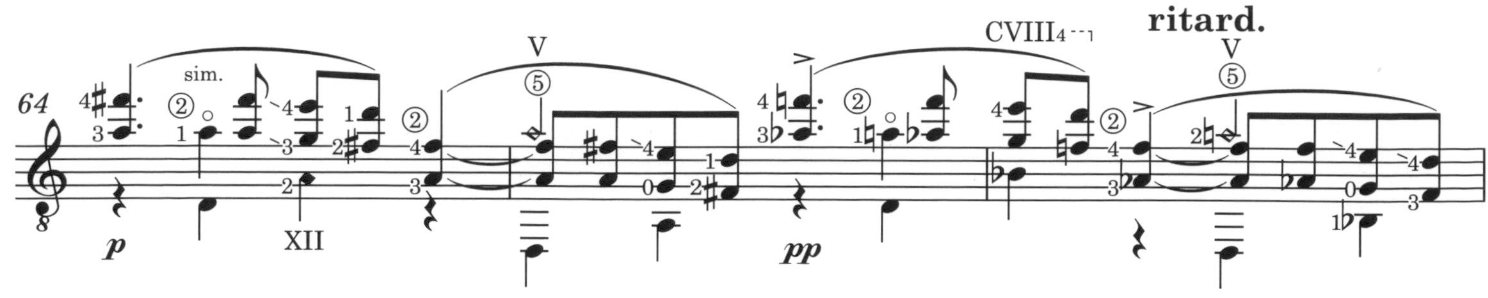

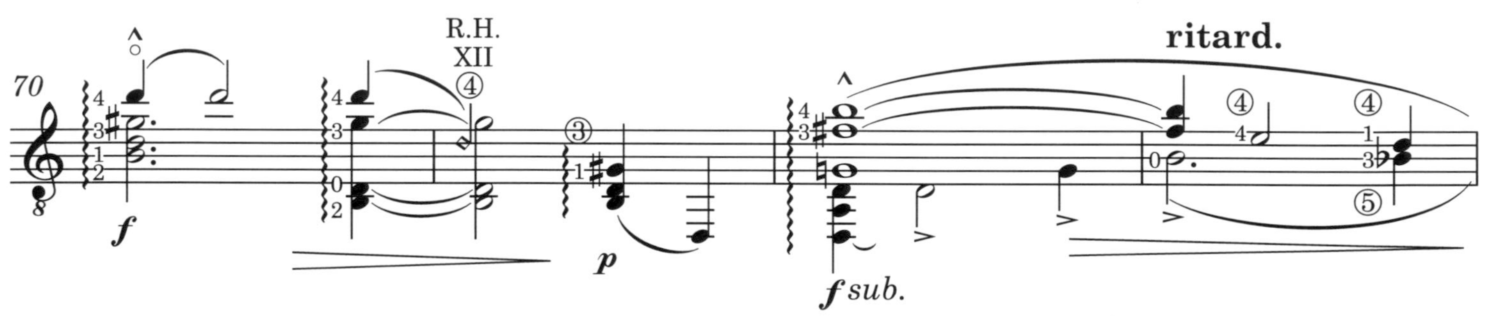

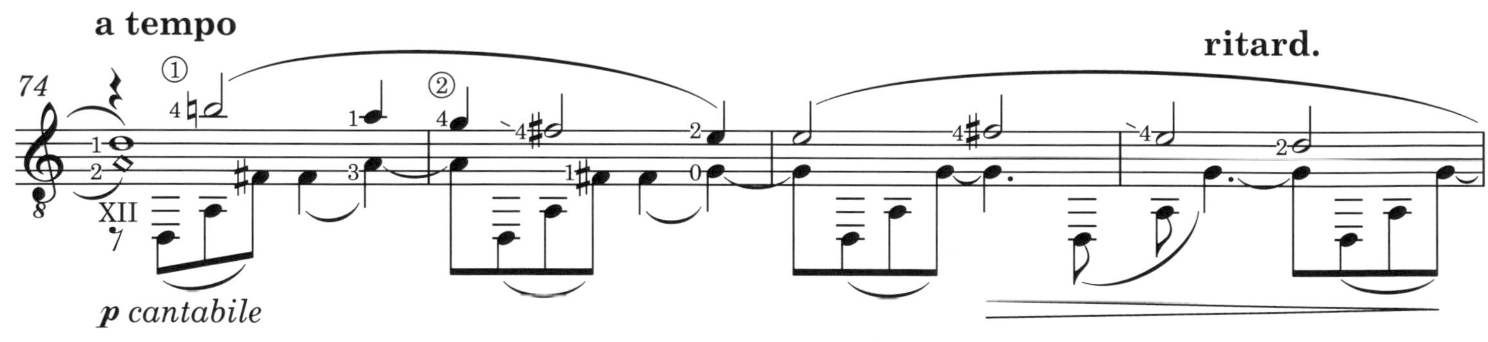

December 20, 2009
1:30 - 5:30 pm
New York City

IV. FLAMENCO FOREVER

Introduction

Allegro appassionato (♩= 120-126)

with fingernails of R.H. on guitar (use a guitar top protector)

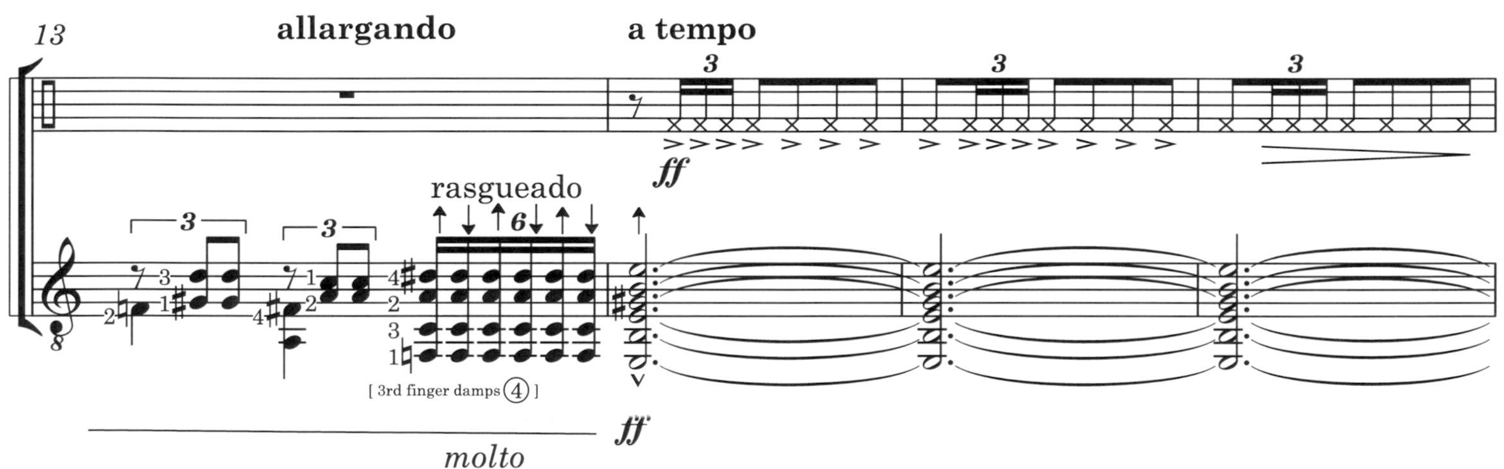

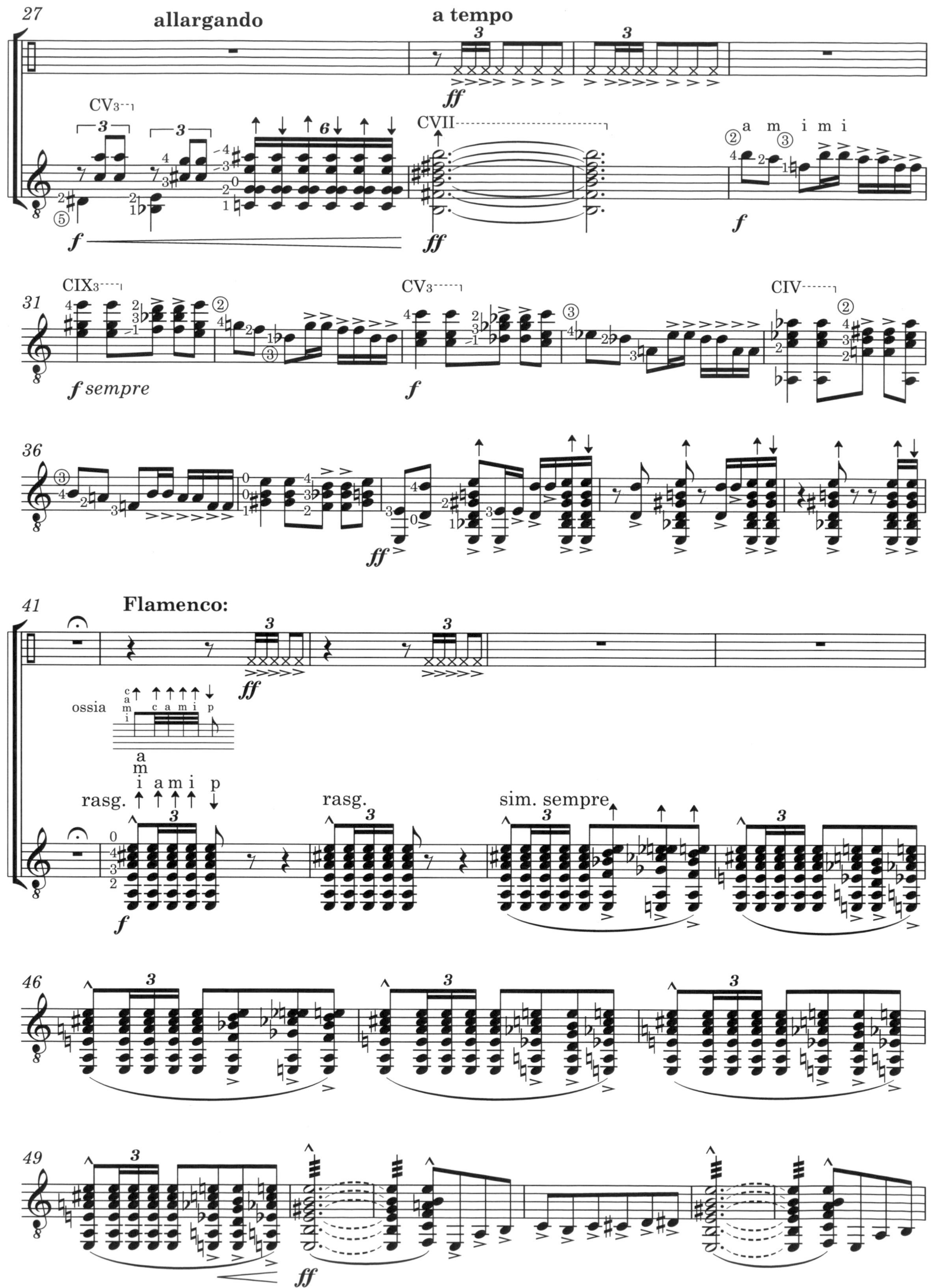
allargando
a tempo
CV3
CVII
a m i m i
CIX3
CV3
CIV
f sempre
Flamenco:
ossia
c a m i p
rasg.
rasg.
sim. sempre

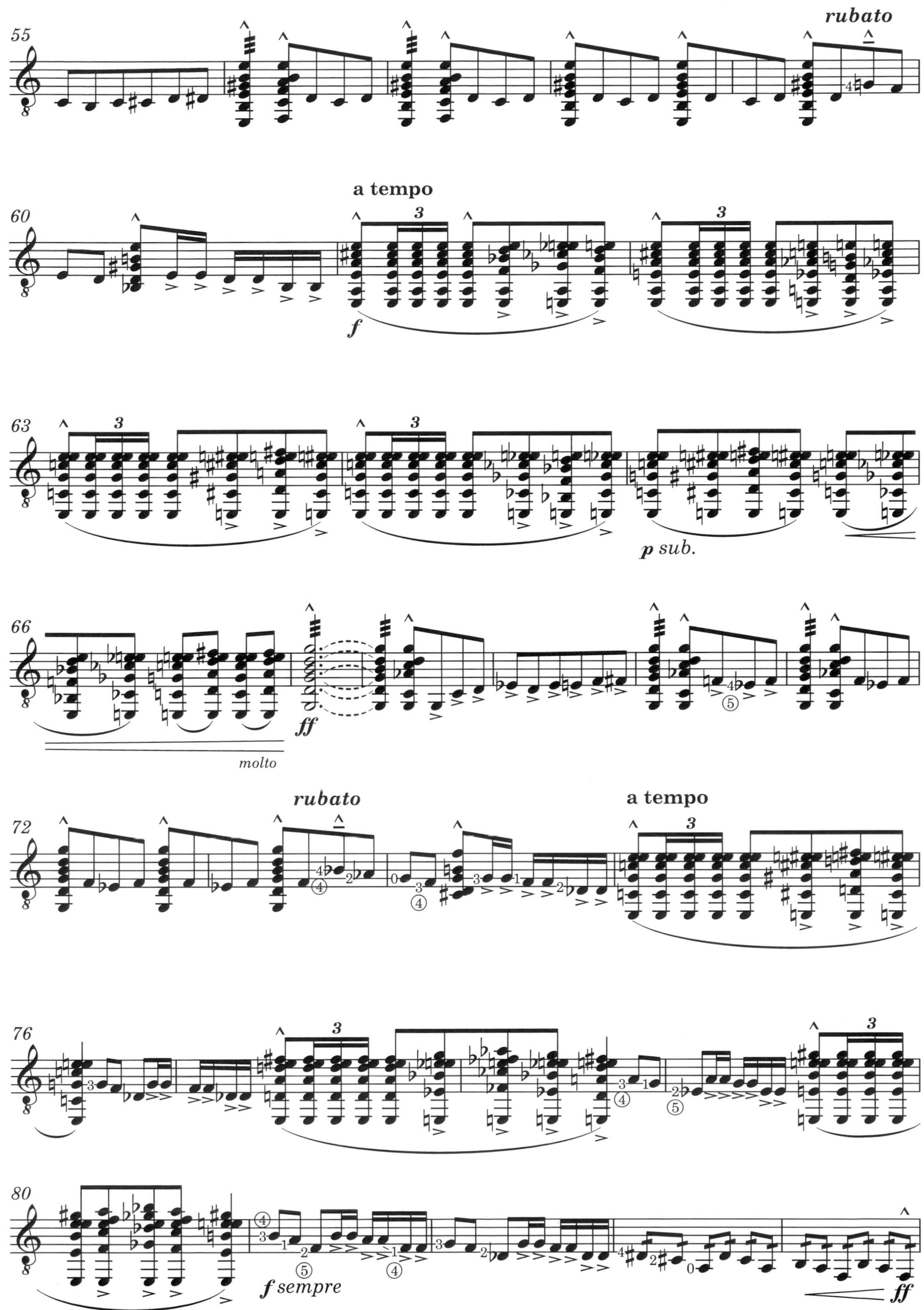

55
rubato
60
a tempo
f
63
p sub.
66
molto
ff
72
rubato
a tempo
76
80
f sempre
ff

Piú mosso (♩= 152)

85
p

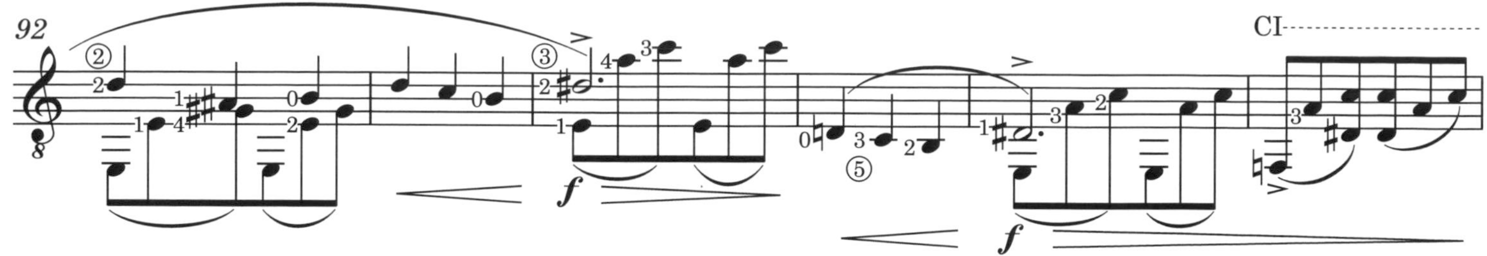
92
CI
f
f

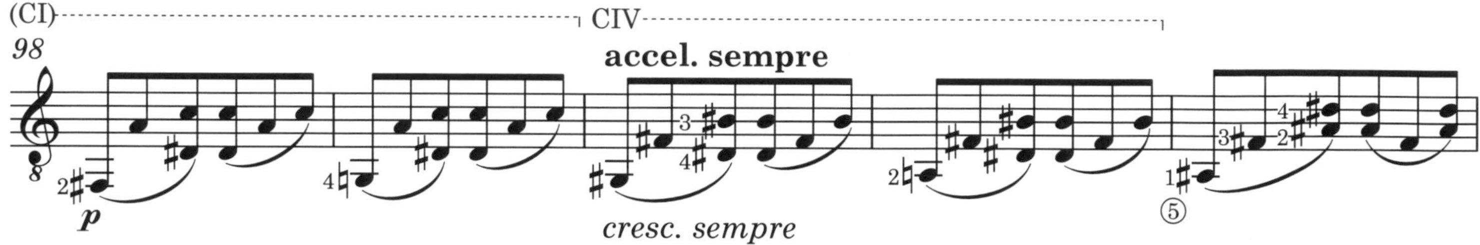
(CI)
CIV
98
accel. sempre
p
cresc. sempre

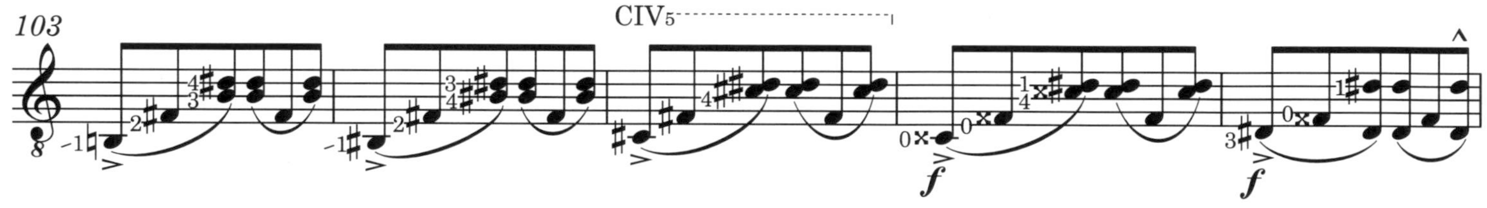
103
CIV5
f
f

108
allarg.
a tempo
p sub.
cresc. molto
f

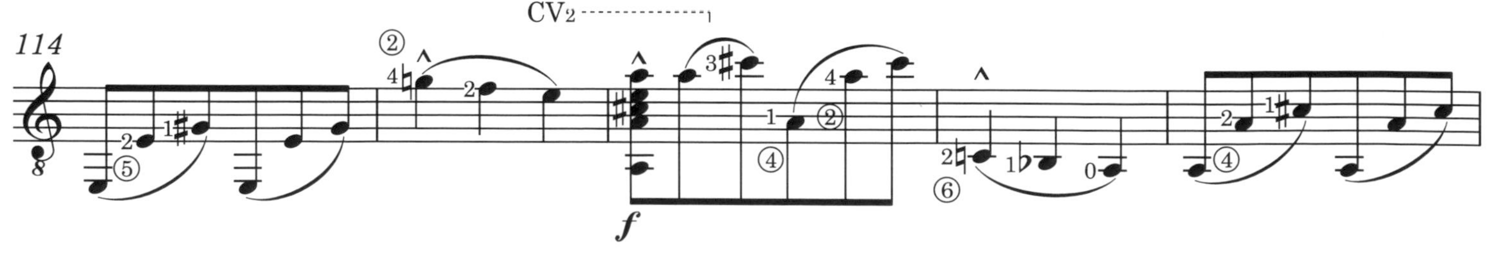
114
CV2
f

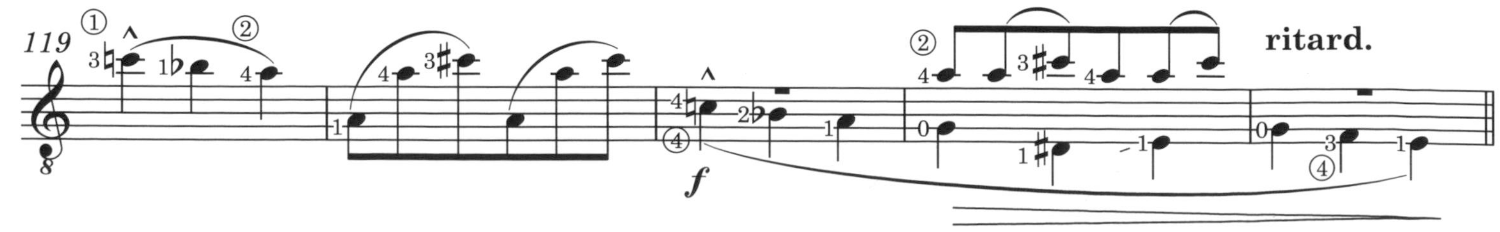
119
ritard.
f

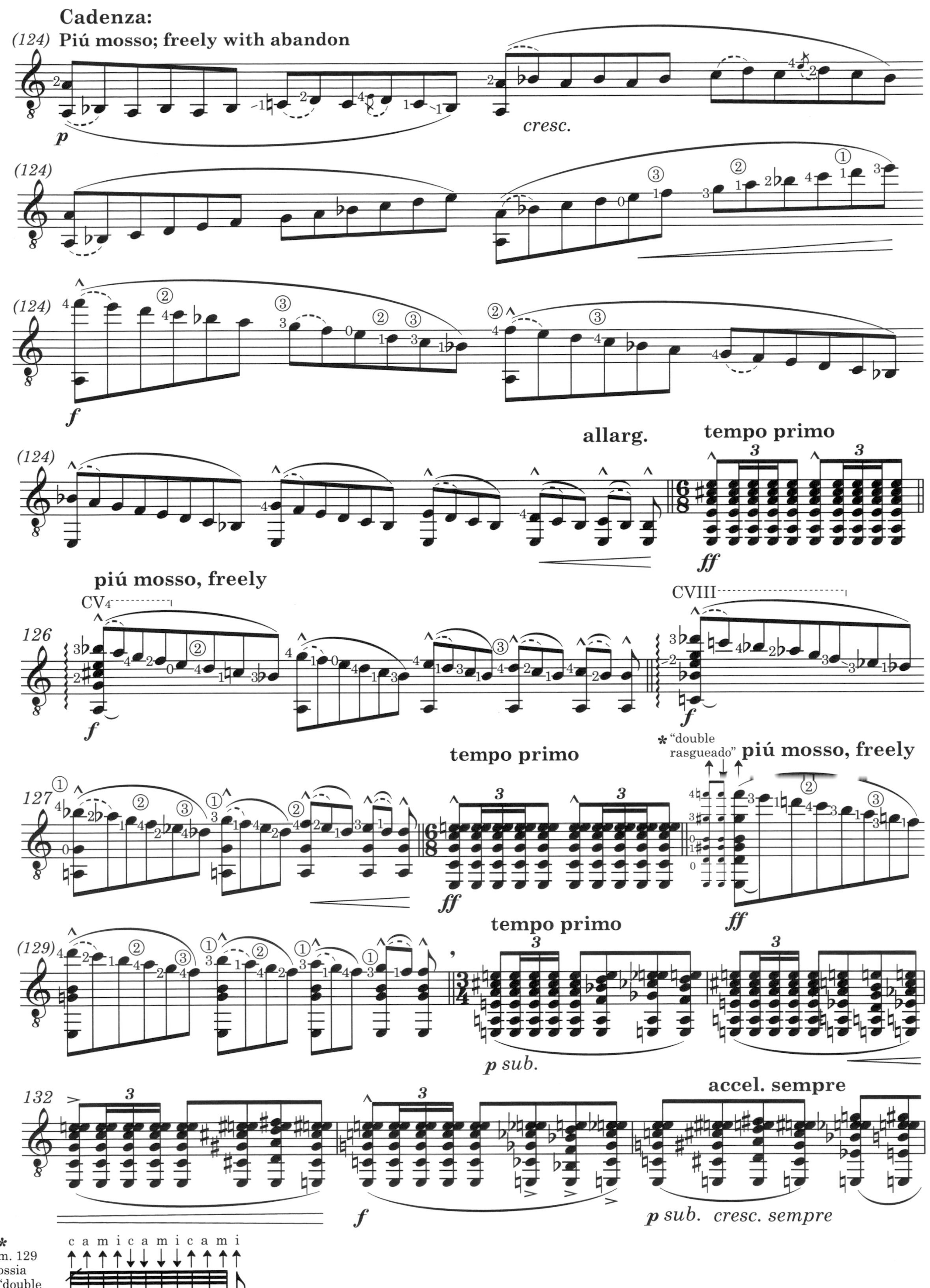

Cadenza:
(124) Piú mosso; freely with abandon
p
cresc.
(124)
(124)
f
(124)
allarg.
tempo primo
ff
piú mosso, freely
CV4
126
f
CVIII
f
tempo primo
* "double rasgueado"
piú mosso, freely
127
ff
ff
(129)
tempo primo
p sub.
132
accel. sempre
f
p sub. cresc. sempre
*
m. 129
ossia
"double rasgueado"
c a m i c a m i c a m i

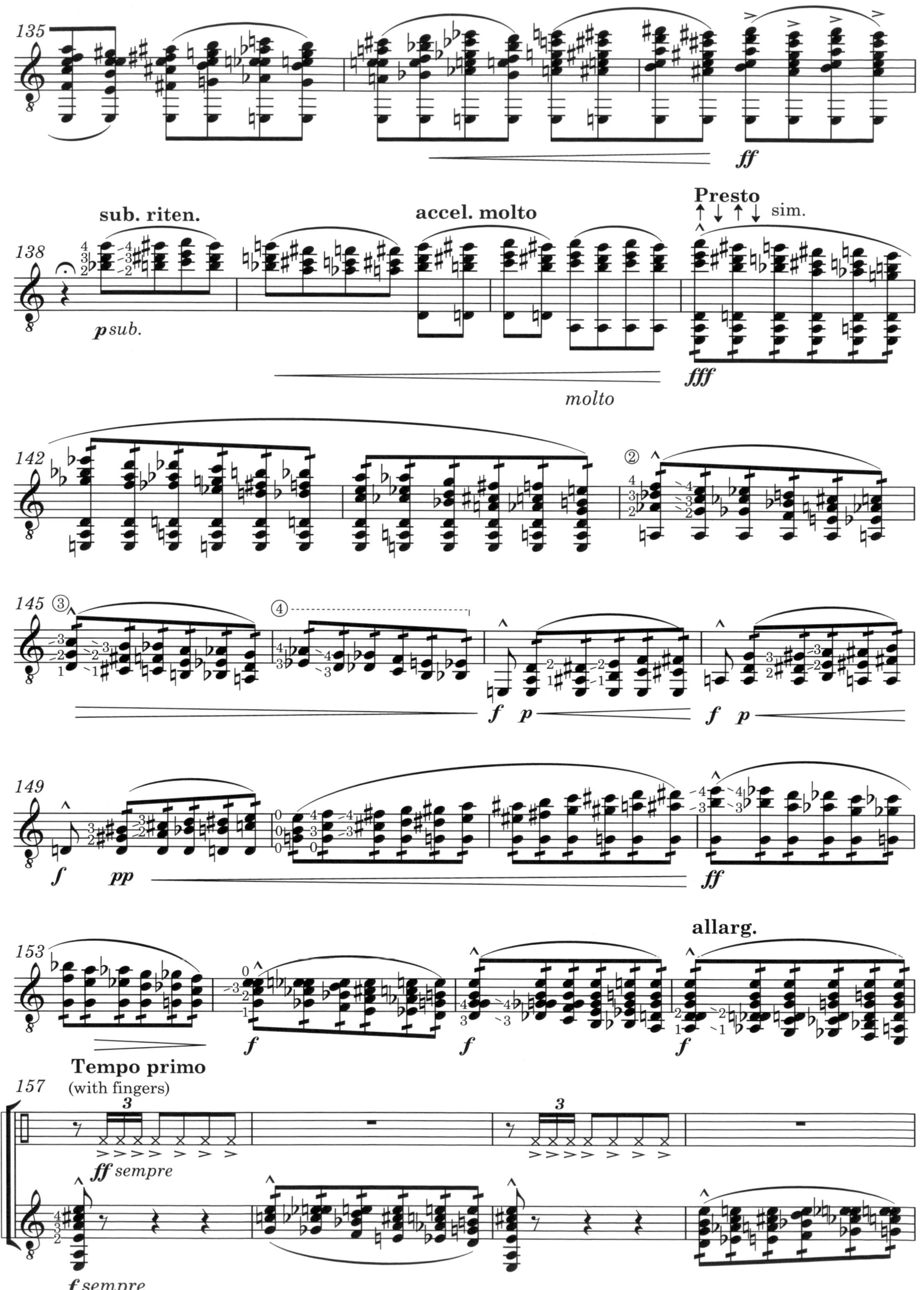
135
ff
sub. riten.
accel. molto
Presto
sim.
138
p sub.
molto
fff
142
145
149
f
p
pp
153
allarg.
Tempo primo
(with fingers)
157
ff sempre
f sempre

161
ff
con bravura
166
p m i
f
ff
f
171
fp
176
ff f
[2th finger damps ③]
180
p
rit.
a tempo
rit.
Meno
mosso
184
p
rit. molto
188

191 **Fugue: Tempo primo** *p* **freely** *f* *p*

196 **a tempo** *ff* *f*

200 **freely** *p* *p* **accel.** **tempo primo**

205 **pesante** **a tempo** *ff* *ff*

210 **freely** *p* **accel.** **a tempo**

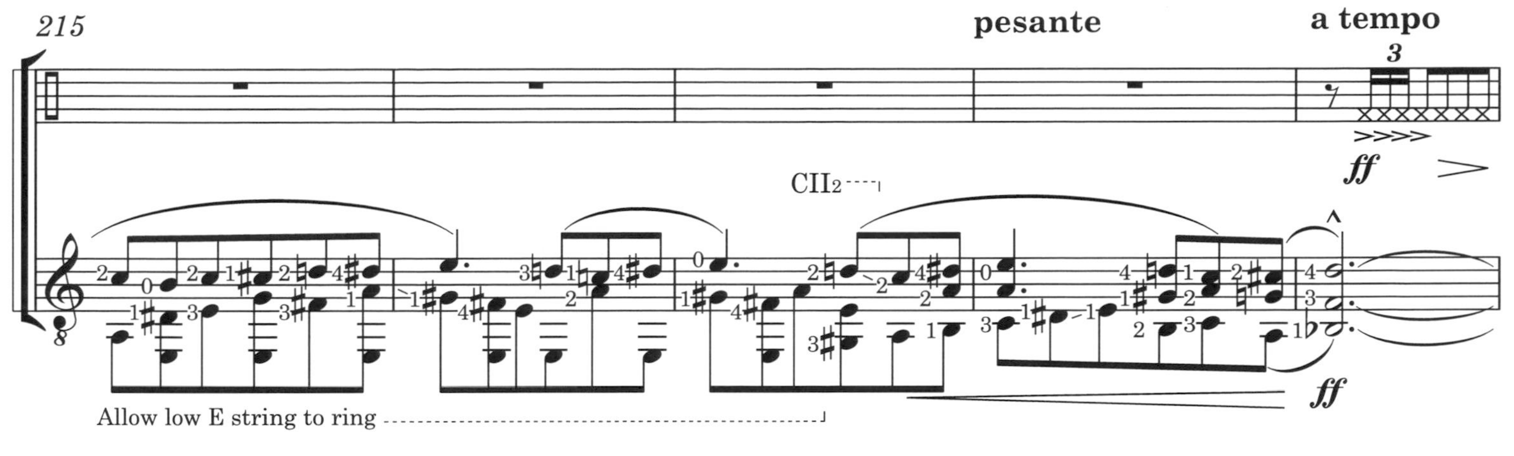
215
pesante
a tempo
3
ff
CII2
Allow low E string to ring
ff

220
freely (meno messo)
p

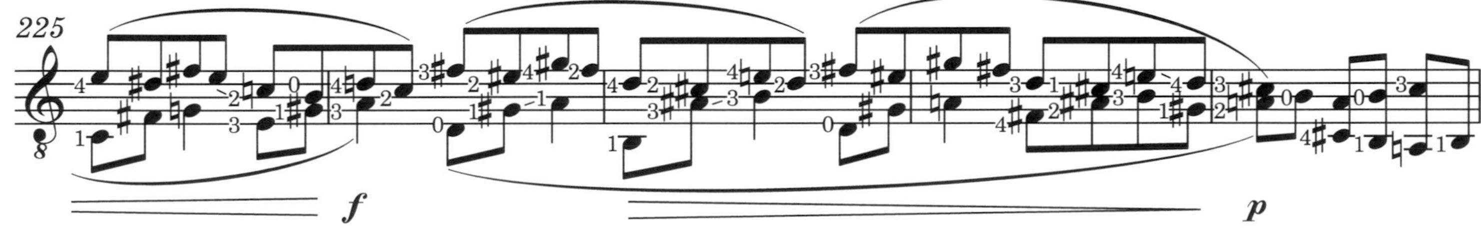
225
f
p

230
Marcato
CI4
cresc. poco a poco

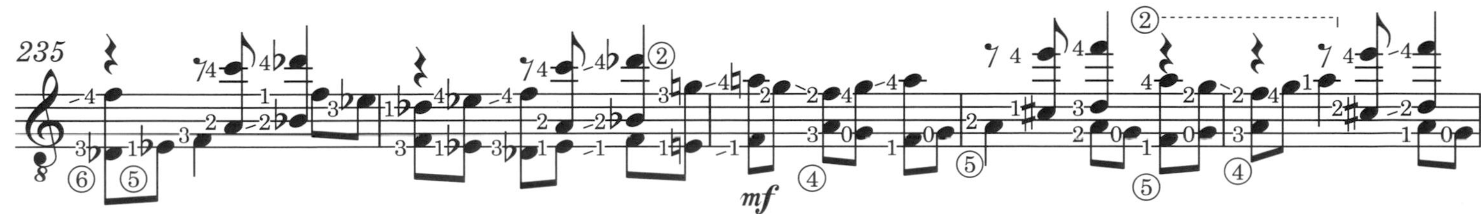
235
mf

240
f

244
CVI4
p
cresc. poco a poco

248
CIX4
CVI3
mf cresc. sempre

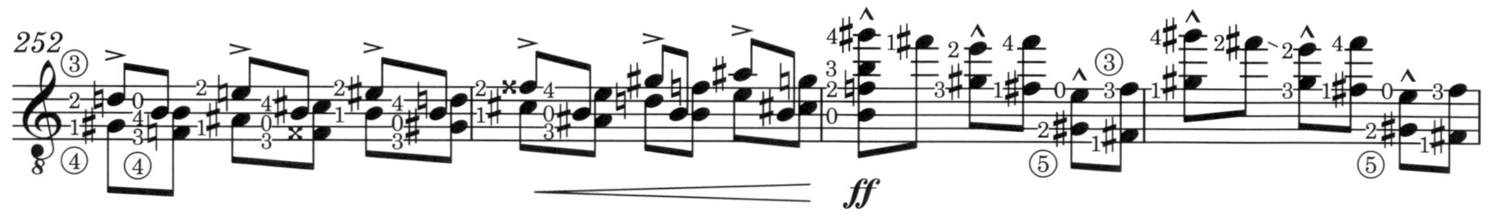
252
ff

256
f
dim.

260
CIII4
rit.
mf

Tempo I, Grazioso
265
p

271 CVII4 CVII4

277 CII4 CVII5 CVII ♮CVII

283 CV2 CIII2 CVIII2

288 CVIII4 CVIII4 CV3 CVIII4

294 *f* *p*

299 *dim.* *p sempre* *pp* *dim.*

304 *mf espr.* *pp*

308
CII4 CI4
CI2
cresc.
313
CI3
318
CIII2
323
CI5
CVII3
CII4 CVII5
329
CVIII4
allarg.
maestoso
rit.
tempo primo
334

339
cresc.

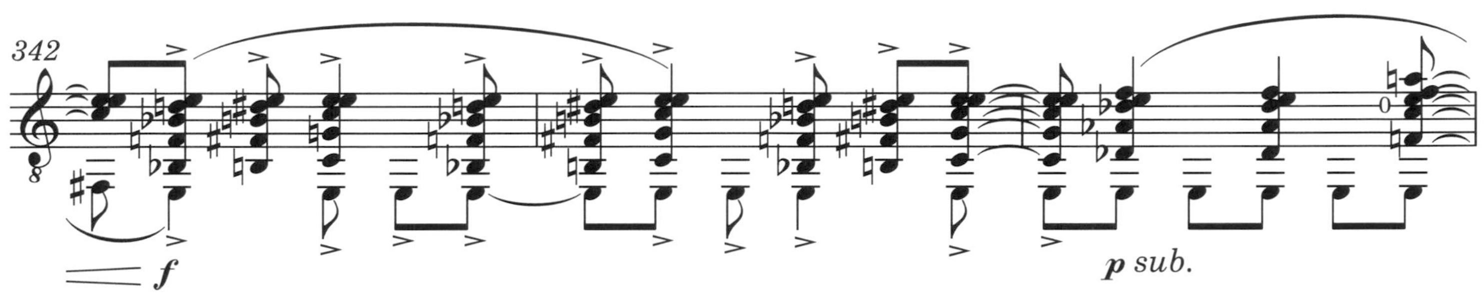
342
f
p sub.

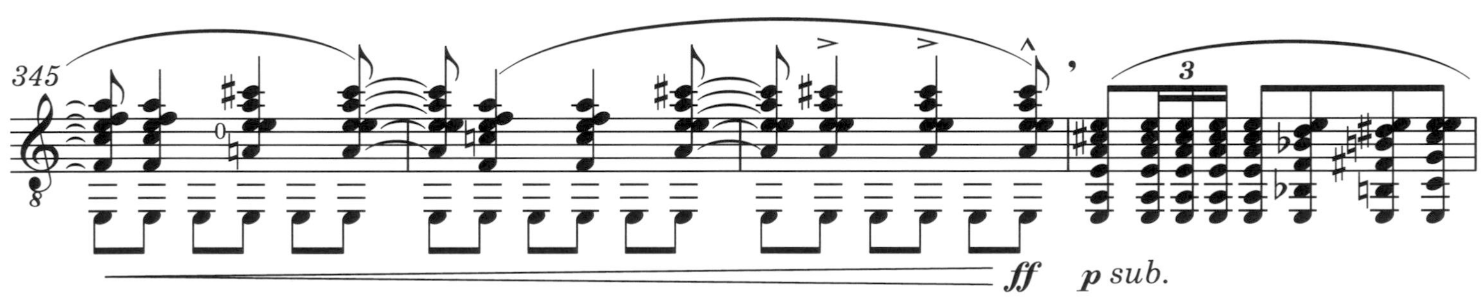
345
ff
p sub.

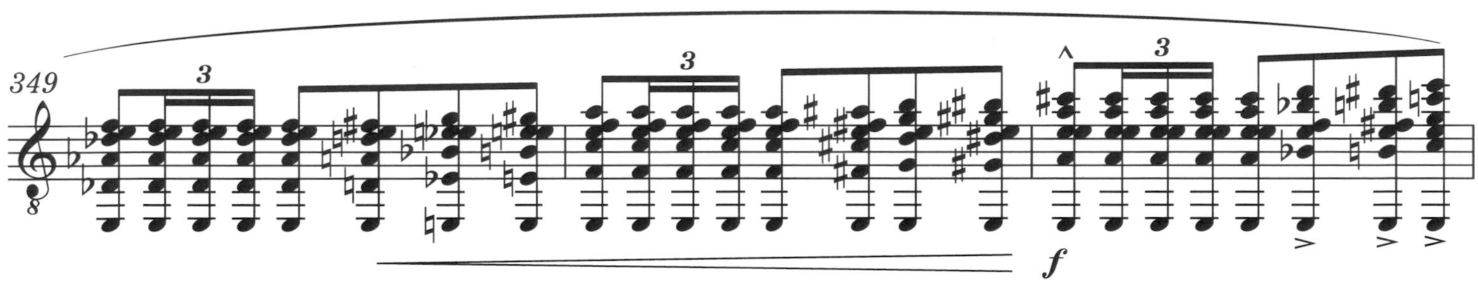
349
f

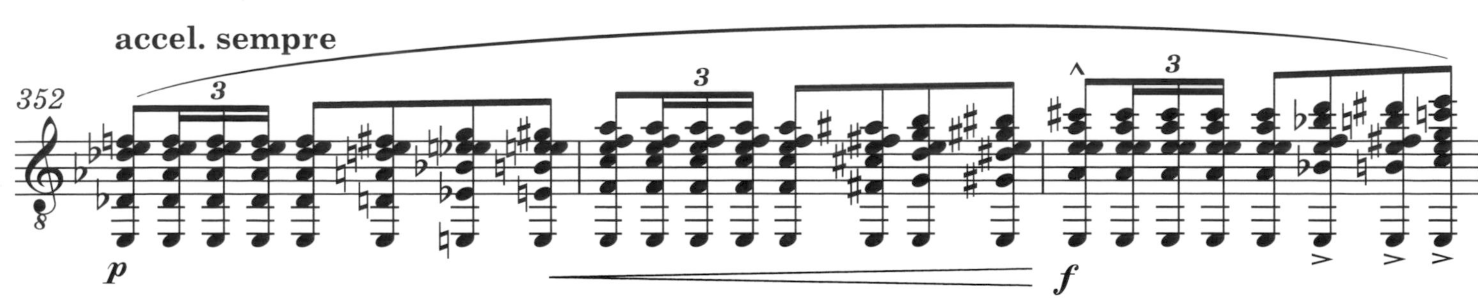
accel. sempre
352
p
f

355
p
cresc.
f
ff
358
sim.
p
molto
Presto
360
fff
363
dim. poco a poco
rit. poco a poco
368
f
CVII2
sempre dim.
mf
CIV2
(rit. poco a poco)
375
CIII2
R.H.
XII
p
Tempo primo
380
with flesh of L.H. fingers. Tap on top of the soundboard near the 12th fret.
mf
8va
V
pp

386
3
3
accel.
f
piú mosso
392
sub. p
cresc. poco a poco
accel. possibile
396
f
400
ff
p sub.
403
406
fff
Presto
fff

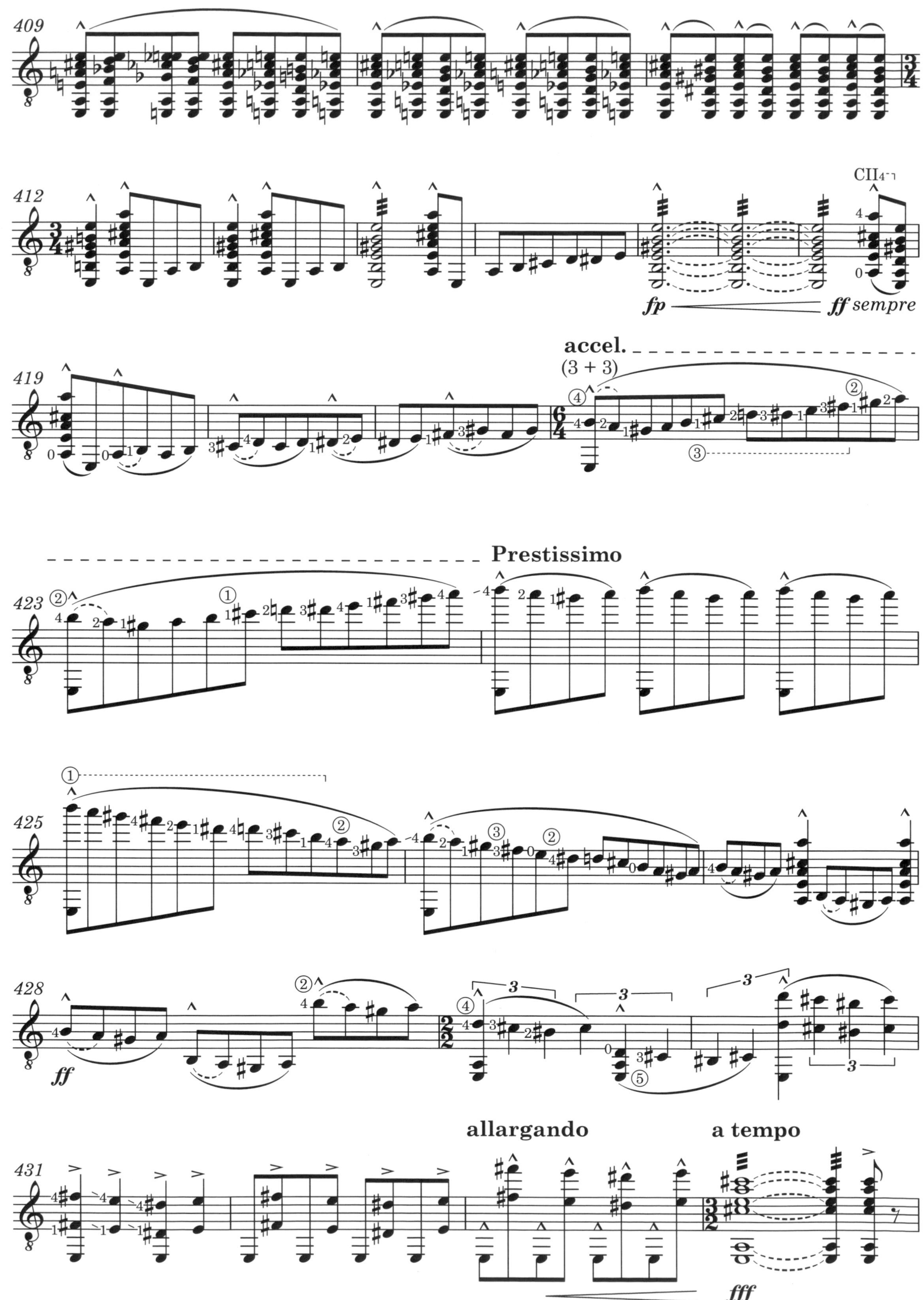
409
412
CII4
fp
ff sempre
419
accel.
(3 + 3)
423
Prestissimo
425
428
ff
431
allargando
a tempo
fff

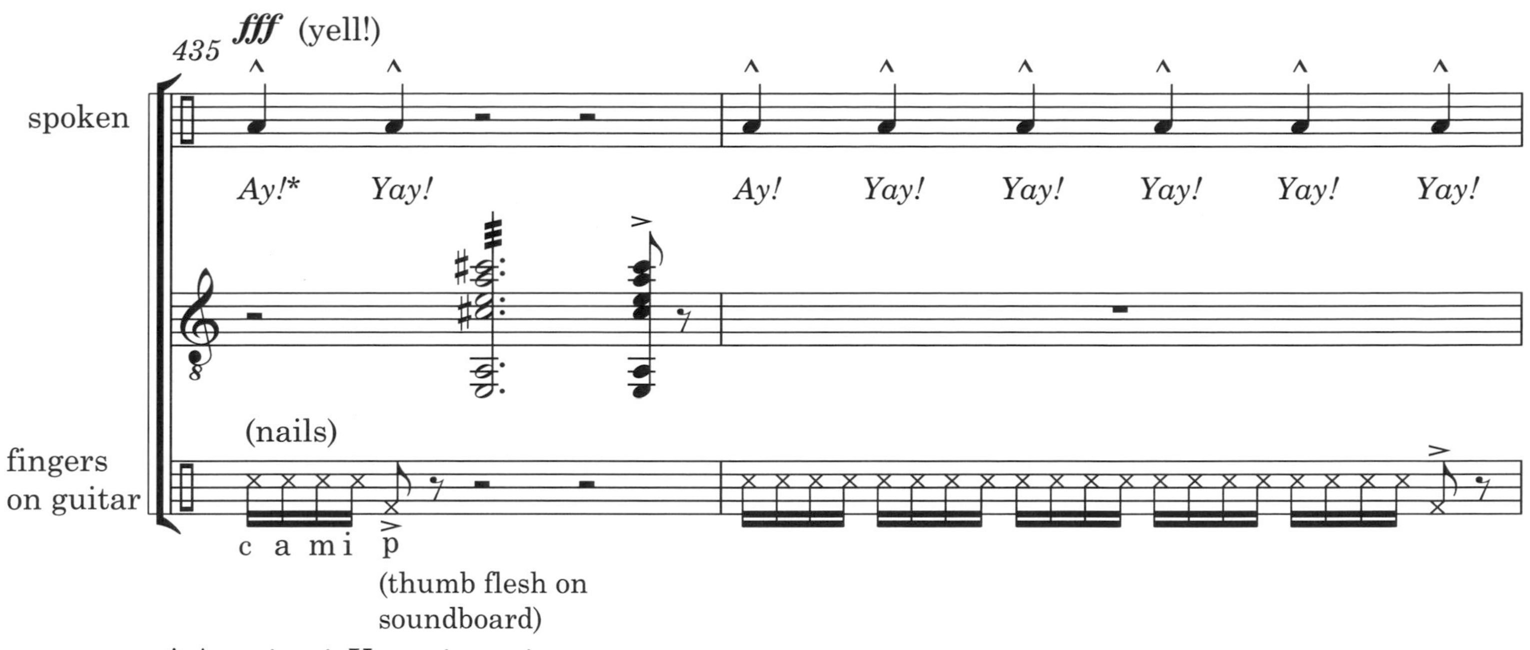

* Ay = 'eye'; Yay = 'y-eye'

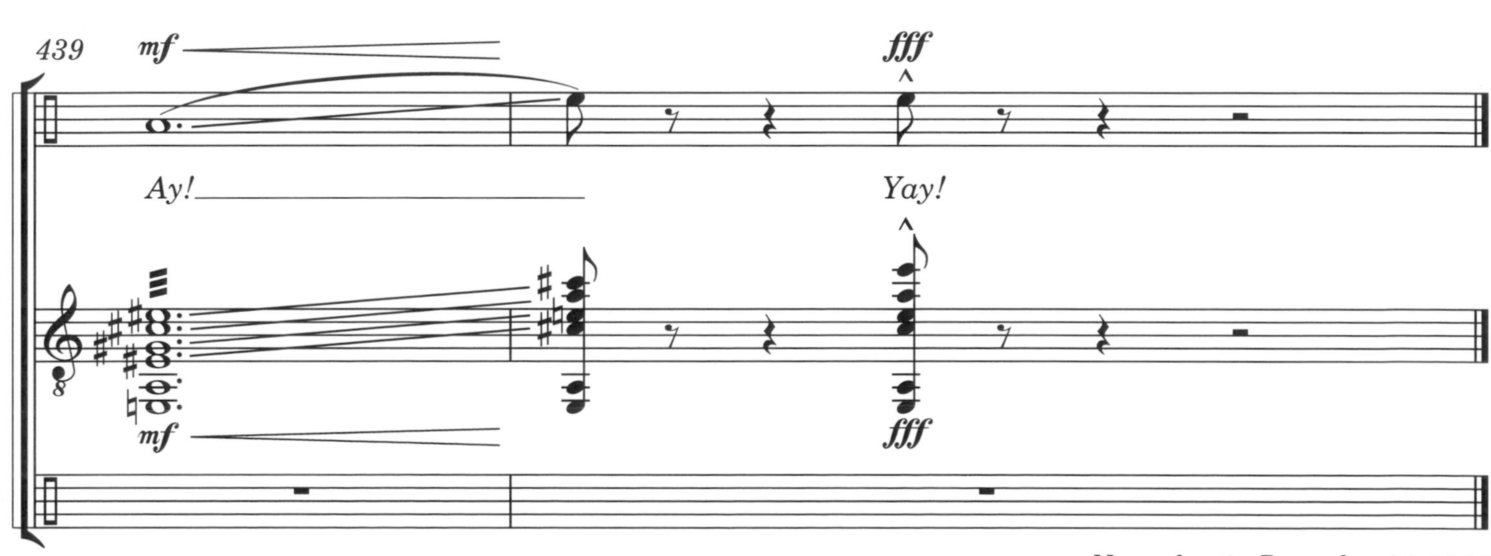

November 1 - December 31, 2009
New York City
revised June 16, 2012